THE
ULTIMATE
KICK

THE ULTIMATE

KICK

THE WALLACE METHOD OF WINNING KARATE

BY BILL "SUPERFOOT" WALLACE

EDITED BY: DAVE CATER
DESIGNED BY: DANILO SILVERIO

UNIQUE PUBLICATIONS
4201 Vanowen Place
Burbank, CA 91505

ISBN: 0-86568-088-4
Library of Congress Catalog Card Number: 86-51504

Please note that the publisher of this instructional book is NOT RESPONSIBLE in any manner whatsoever for any injury which may occur by reading and/or following the instructions herein.

It is essential that before following any of the activities, physical or otherwise, herein described, the reader or readers should first consult his or her physician for advice on whether or not the reader or readers should embark on the physical activity described herein. Since the physical activities described herein may be too sophisticated in nature, it is ESSENTIAL THAT A PHYSICIAN BE CONSULTED.

CONTENTS

PROLOGUE

It was early in his professional full-contact boxing career that Bill Wallace took time out from a rigorous training schedule to attend a Los Angeles Lakers basketball game with his manager Don Quine. Wallace could enjoy this moment away from the training hall because he had just knocked out an opponent with a powerful roundhouse kick to the face.

Midway through the game, Quine went to get something to eat. Above the food stand a sign read, "Super foot long hot dogs."

"Wow," Quine would say later as he returned to his seat, "that would be a great nickname for you." Wallace was not immediately enamored by the new tag. Though he called it "dumb and hokey," he added, "as nicknames go, I kind of liked it."

The easy part was editing the advertisement to fit the fighter. The hard part was getting the fighter to prove he was more than just the product of a manager's overzealous promotional scheme.

Most observers wondered if he could live up to the name "Superfoot." What they didn't know, however, was that Wallace had been proving himself for years by living well past the life expectancy of a fighter with a decided handicap.

Late in 1966, Wallace suffered torn ligaments in his right knee while studying judo. When he began karate training several months later, he found that the injury prohibited him from using his right leg. A spinning kick, a front kick, any movement coming from the right was useless.

Thus, Wallace employed a method of fighting left side forward. It was a technique that many observers considered suicide. All an opponent would have to do is get Wallace to switch sides, to fight from an alien angle and the fighter would disintegrate.

But Wallace proved the experts wrong. He discovered that through a fanatical training regimen he could learn to fend off any attacks against his weaker side. When he fought, he fought left side forward. When he fell or was knocked down (which seldom occurred) he sprang up left side forward. What others could do with two sides, Wallace accomplished with one side.

And he won, 23 times as a professional without a loss (two exhibition wins are not included in the official record).

Today, well into professional kickboxing retirement, Wallace ranks among the top speakers on the martial arts seminar circuit. Young practitioners marvel at his flexibility, the way he can still shoot his left leg to the sky. They flock to his seminars to hear how he turned a major weakness into an unbeatable strength.

But most of all they come to borrow, to steal, to copy a bit of the Wallace mystique that has kept him on top well past his fighting years.

The Wallace method to winning karate is more than a well-placed roundhouse kick or a jab to an off-balance opponent. It is a total fighting philosophy, a way of survival both in and out of the ring. It is Bill Wallace at his unmasked best.

It is *The Ultimate Kick*, a comprehensive look at the techniques of the only man who could live up to the name "Superfoot."

THE WALLACE METHOD

I fight the way I fight because I had to. I hurt my right leg (torn ligaments) in a judo accident in 1966 and started karate in 1967. When I hurt my right leg, I all but lost the use of it as far as karate was concerned. It became a base, a foundation and nothing more.

So what I decided to do was fight left-legged and left-handed. Since I was always a kicker, I decided to stay left side forward in a side horse stance because in the shorin-ryu system, that's how we fought. I kept my left hand low because I didn't want to get hit in the ribs. I was quick enough with my awareness that I could get out of the way of a punch to my head, a backfist or a kick. When I started fighting, I had a side kick, a front leg roundhouse kick low and a backfist. That was it — three basic techniques. As I progressed, I decided I needed more kicks, especially if a guy was charging at me. So I developed a hook kick, again with the forward leg. All three kicks were done with the forward leg.

I continue to fight the way I've always fought because it works for me. I had the speed where I could flip the little roundhouse kick up to the opponent's tummy and nobody could block it.

Despite the many different fighters I've faced and the many challenges I've had, I have not changed my fighting since 1967. And the reason is that it's natural to me. I kick with my left leg and punch with my left hand. When I fight sideways, I am very comfortable simply because I know I'm fairly well-protected. I don't want to get hit. Who does? I want to defend myself and I want to defend myself in the best possible position. If you attack me, it is very easy for me to bend over sideways. Consequently, it is also easy for me to attack sideways. I can run at you, especially from a short distance, because I'm protecting myself as I come. I don't ever remember running into a punch. Whatever way, I'm controlled. I never lose sight of where I've been or where I'm going.

This is just one way, my way of doing something. Obviously, my success over the years says I have been doing something right. But remember: We're all built differently. We all have different strengths and weaknesses. But above all we have different psychological makeups. My makeup is even though I'm standing right next to you where it would be easy for me to punch you in the face, I'd rather kick you. That makes me feel good, it helps my ego and makes you look bad in my mind; because Wallace kicked you even though you knew Wallace was going to kick you.

MY KICKING
PHILOSOPHY

I only have three kicks — the side kick, the roundhouse kick and the hook kick — but they come at you from so many different angles you'd swear I had 20 kicks in my arsenal.

The side kick can work into a roundhouse kick, the side kick can work into a hook kick. Remember: Since they all come at you in the same way, you can't tell what the kick will be until the leg is straight. And hopefully, by the time you finally realize what the kick is, you won't have time to react.

The only avenue to good reaction is through sparring. I am lucky; I love to work out and I love to spar. I'll spar white belts, beginning students, brand new black belts, street fighters and world champions. The only true way to learn, the only way you'll know if your kicking techniques are any good is through sparring. That's the ultimate.

You can do all the forms you want, learn all the techniques and master the self-defense movements, but when you're sparring, that's when your kicking speed, power, timing and distance come in. That is what karate is for me. It's a martial art and "martial" means a warring type art.

Because of my leg problem, I had to get what you might call "sneaky." Everybody knew the roundhouse kick was coming, everybody knew the side kick was coming, everybody knew the hook kick was coming. But the trick for an opponent was to determine which one it was and where it would land.

You see, most people turn their hips when they're performing a hook kick. I don't. When most people throw a side kick they turn their hips because they can't get their knee high enough. I don't. When most people execute a roundhouse kick, they point their knee at the opponent. Once the knee points at your opponent, he knows the knee has to come around.

My three kicks come from the same position, from the same chambering action. You never know what is happening. And I don't know what's happening. All I do is step in for the kick and watch how you react to what you think is coming. I react to your movement.

Wallace's method takes advantage of an opponent who is off balance. From the ready position (1), Wallace throws a roundhouse kick (2), which is thwarted when the defender leans away (3). As the defender comes forward to counterpunch (4), Wallace retaliates with a hook kick (5), then catches the defender in the face (6).

Wallace leans from a roundhouse kick (1), coils for the strike (2) and connects with a hook kick (3-4).

From a ready position (1), the defender manages to jam
Wallace's kick (2). Wallace counters (3) with a hook kick
(4).

From a ready position (1), Wallace counters a leg sweep
(2) by leaning back and taking the weight off his front
leg (3). He then counters with a defensive hook kick
(4).

To make the fake sweep work (1), you have to touch your opponent's rear leg. Here the fake works because the opponent moves back to brace for the sweep (2) and then is hit with a hook kick (3).

Different angles of kicks.

Faking is as much a part of Wallace's repertoire as kicking. In this example (1), Wallace fakes a hook kick (2) and as the defender goes to block the kick with his left arm (3), Wallace recoils (4) and delivers a roundhouse kick to the side of the head (5).

Using a chair as a support, Wallace shows how you easily can practice exercises that offer balance, strength and
training. He suggests practicing the kicks slowly to
develop technique, strength and endurance.

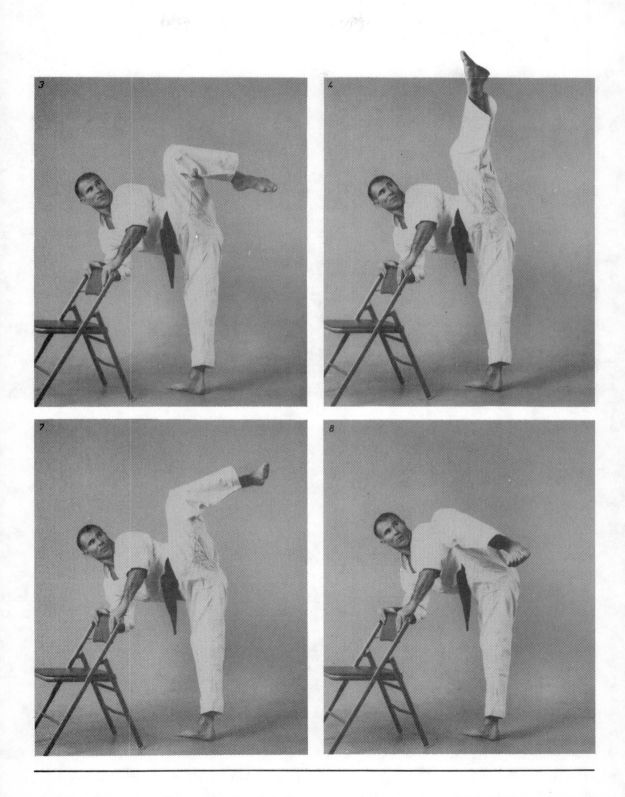

From a ready position (1), the attacker throws a backfist (2). But Wallace leans back (3) to avoid the punch and catches his opponent off balance with a hook kick (4).

Using a left side forward stance (1), Wallace fakes a sweep (2-3), forcing the defender to counter. He then recoils (4) and begins to execute a side kick to the defender's right leg.

By making the opponent think low (1), you can easily
strike with a high kick to the head (2).

In this example of a basic block (1-2), the defender has
made the necessary move. But any good counterattacker
will seize the opening to score.

From a ready position (1), Wallace begins what appears to be a low kick (2). Notice the right hand of the defender has come down to block the strike (3). However, Wallace recoils and applies a hook kick (4) to the side of the head (5).

In this sequence, Wallace works his opponent to perfection (1-6) moving first low then high, then low and high again with a kick to thwart any chance for a counter. Wallace works on the theory that his real move will depend on how his opponent reacts to the fakes at the outset of the technique. The roundhouse high, therefore, easily connects to the side of the head.

Sometimes it takes more than one punch to gain an opening. In this example, Wallace throws (1) a low roundhouse kick to his opponent's groin, creating an opening as the guard is lowered. He then attacks (2) with a backfist that is partially blocked. They return (3) to the fighting position and then Wallace uncorks another backfist (4). As the defender reacts (5), Wallace comes in with a side kick underneath the backfist for a score (6).

In this example of a sliding roundhouse kick (1), as the
defender goes for the block (2), Wallace deftly moves
into a scoring hook kick (3).

As the defender assumes a fighting stance, Wallace drives a side kick (1) into his immobilized arm. As the arm is lowered, he can either send a roundhouse kick into the face (2) or a hook kick to the side of the head.

Wallace is an exponent of executing several techniques to set up the real killer. In this sequence, he attempts a side kick to the arm, which causes the defender to keep it close to his body (1). He then recoils (2), and seizes the opening for a hook kick (3-4). He pulls back the kick (5) and delivers (6) a shot to the midsection. Again he pulls back his leg (7) and returns to a stationary fighting position (8).

As Wallace throws a roundhouse kick to the arm (1), he creates an opening for a high roundhouse kick to the head (2-3). By first going to the arm, Wallace leaves himself with several options. He can either use a stomach/outside of the head combination (4-5) or a stomach/inside of the head strike (6-7).

The side kick is one of the basic fighting techniques. However, its use can have long-lasting effects. In this example, Wallace applies a side kick (1-2), which causes the defender to lower his guard. Wallace then comes with a right punching combination to the face (3-5) and a left to the midsection (6).

Although you're close to your opponent, you can still score if you use the Wallace method. From this close-in position (1), Wallace raises the kick (2) and scores to the head (3).

The Wallace method (1-3) of raising the knee for protection. Also shown is the front view. Notice the knee is high for protection (4).

Jamming an opponent can be an effective counter. From
a fighting stance (1), Wallace leans back (2) to avoid
what looks to be the beginning of a kicking movement.
He counters (3) immediately with a hook kick. As the
defender is about to step into his kick (4), Wallace steps
in to jam the movement (5-6).

From a ready stance (1), the attacker attempts to throw a kick (2). But Wallace jams the move (3) and applies a quick hook kick. The opponent leans back to avoid the kick as Wallace recoils (4). He then finishes off his opponent with another defensive hook kick to the face (5).

FOOTWORK
AND STANCES

My footwork has always been considered phenomenal in a way because I take short little snappy movements rather than long slow cumbersome steps.

Since kicking is my bread and butter, I don't want to expose myself and telegraph my techniques, so short steps give me the flexibility of seeing my opponent while still maintaining enough movement to get out of the way. If I'm moving forward, I step with my left leg first. If I'm moving backward, I step with my rear leg.

When speaking of footwork and stances, it is wise to remember the importance of both offense *and* defense. A fighter can be too offensive minded or too defensive minded, but a keen awareness of the two can keep you on your feet much longer.

Obviously, there is a big difference in being either offensive or defensive in nature. For instance, if I throw a roundhouse kick defensively, I don't have to change anything. I just don't have the time. If I throw a hook kick defensively, I don't want to have to turn, again because I don't have the time. Also, with the sidestance, I've taken most of your targets away. Most of the targets are no longer in front of you so you have to come around. And that leaves you open to attack. When it comes to blocking technique, I'd rather defend an area than try to stop one blow. If I see you're going to throw a roundhouse kick, I don't protect against the kick. I'll protect an area, whether it is the side of my face, chest or stomach. I let my arms do the blocking; I don't raise them, I just turn to where the target is no longer in your line of sight or where it is no longer available to you.

The stance I primarily use is the horse stance or modified horse stance. It is not so deep as it is wide — about two shoulder widths. I still want to have my center of gravity high enough so that I can have very quick, very influential, very rhythmic type movements. My stepping movement is simply a step, slide and kick.

All three kicking movements — the side kick, the roundhouse and the hook kick — come from the same stepping movements. The backfist comes from the same stepping movement and the hook punch, if used offensively, comes from the same movement.

Very simply, my chief goal was never to get hit. Pain hurts, it ruins your whole day. You have to work toward protecting yourself during all phases of a contest. Only by maintaining the proper footwork and stances can you keep yourself covered while creating openings in your opponent. Whatever I do, I want to make sure he cannot counter it and return the favor. I always want to be in the proper position to block an attack after a block. Only through proper footwork and stances can this be attained.

Leaning defense against a high kick. From a basic fighting stance (1), the opponent blocks a low hook kick (2) and then a high hook kick (3).

The key is to keep something between you and the opponent. It can be distance, an arm or a leg. Wallace prefers to protect an area, rather than block a specific technique. In this sequence, he shows how blocks transpire from a basic fighting stance (1). There is a defense against a side kick (2), a hook kick (3) and three defenses against a roundhouse kick (4-6) using the upper, inside and lower portions of the arm.

In defending against a straight punch (1-2), there is no need to touch your opponent. A simple movement backward staves any attack.

From a fighting stance (1), the defender can either lean away from the punch (2) or use a high traditional block (3).

Wallace contends the front arm or hand is useless
because it was never taught to do anything. And so it
never really protects anything. For it to protect something it has to move, and by moving it creates openings.

No matter how far the attacker moves from a basic
stance (1), Wallace can lean away from the attack (2-3).
Only his arm accepts punishment.

Here are two examples of defending against a front kick. The traditional version (1) shows a basic downward block. Notice the opening the block has created in the midsection. By using Wallace's method (2), the arm is down and absorbs the blow. By leaning back, Wallace has kept his body closed to attack.

Again from a basic stance (1), the defender has blocked the side kick with his arm (2) while not jeopardizing the rest of his defenses.

Leaning from a body punch.

A little jamming action can go a long way toward neutralizing your opponent. In this example (1), Wallace uses his left leg to jam his opponent's right leg (2-3) and follows with a backfist to the face (4).

Once the traditional bow has been made (1-2), keep an eye on which way your opponent moves. It could help you win the match.

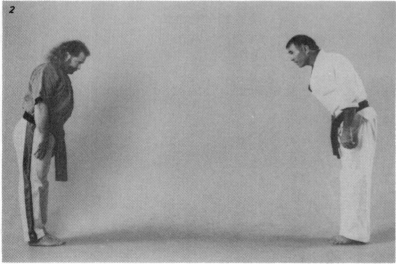

What can you notice about these stances (1-2)? Notice the hand position, the stance, the expected hip movement and the foot position.

This is a close-up of how Wallace leans his head and body out of the way of an incoming strike.

These are ways of leaning from an opponent's attack. Notice at no time does the right hand move from the chin. Also, the left arm is always between Wallace and the other fighter.

Just having the right stance or hand position is not
always enough. The defender must also move to avoid
getting hit. In this example (1), Wallace has little trouble
reaching his opponent with a kick to the midsection (2)
or the head (3).

Starting from various stances (1-3), Wallace shows how
a fighter can move into a kick, stop himself by using a
defense and then counterattack (4-8).

Even though the defender has her arms raised, she is not
very well protected. Wallace can reach her with a right
(1) or left (2) hook punch to the midsection, a right jab
to the head or face (3) or a left jab to the face (4).

By leaning away from a punch (1), you can keep your opponent off balance and relatively ineffective (2). His defenses in disarray (3), he is an easy target for a counter side kick.

As the attack is made (1), Wallace leans back and forces his opponent off balance (2). Thus, he is easy prey for a countering ridgehand (3).

Whether you use the right or left hand, hook punches (1-3) can provide the power you may be missing.

Facing a regular karate stance, Wallace shows how he takes advantage of openings (1-3) in the stomach, head and groin areas.

If you happen to be facing a Korean stylist, many of the same openings apply, including the upper ribs (1), the chest (2), the groin (3) and the lower abdomen (4). Each opening is created by throwing techniques not so much to score, but to set up powerful combinations.

As Wallace's opponent takes a boxing style stance, he jams a side kick into his chest and arms (1). This causes him to pull in his arms. With the arms immobilized, he works a hook kick to the side of the head (2) and then the face (3). The guard comes up and he throws a side kick (4) under the elbows. He cocks his leg (5) and the game begins again (6).

In a boxing stance (1), the defender is hit with a side kick
to the chest (2). He is forced to pull his arms down (3).
The force of the blow causes the defender to bend over
(4), making him vulnerable to a kick to the head (5).

From the boxing fighting position, Wallace shows the
different openings available to an attacker. The back (1),
the side (2), the midsection (3), the upper chest area (4),
the ribs (5) and the side of the head (6).

Throwing a side kick to the upper arm area (1) or the chin (2) forces the arms in and creates an opening in the lower chest area, as Wallace shows (3). Thus, the scoring technique is easily executed (4).

From a Korean fighting stance (1), the defender must move his forward hand down to block the kick out (2) or up to block the kick in (3).

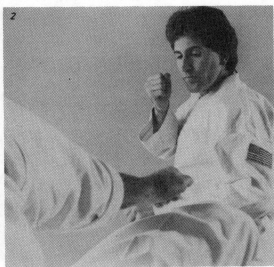

In this sequence, Wallace throws a roundhouse kick to set up a reverse punch to the face. From a fighting stance (1), he cocks the leg (2) and applies a roundhouse kick to the defender's stomach (3). He recoils (4), and while the opponent is still reeling from the earlier blow, he adds a punishing reverse punch to the face (5-6).

Facing a fighter in a Korean stance (1), Wallace throws a
backfist at face level (2). As the defender brings up his
left hand to block the blow (3) Wallace recoils (4) and
executes a scoring hook kick to the face (5).

Setting up an opponent is not that difficult against a fighter in a boxing stance. Here, Wallace opens with a roundhouse kick (1) to the stomach. He recoils (2) and snaps the kick again under his elbow guards (3). As the fighter drops to protect against another attack to the midsection (4), Wallace crosses him up and kicks to the face (5).

As the defender pulls in (1) his elbows, Wallace fakes (2) a side kick low (3) into the stomach. Wallace counters the move by bringing his leg across (4-7) and throwing a hook kick to the side of the head. The extension of the hook kick is shown from a side view (8). However, if the hook kick misses, he can come back with a roundhouse kick (9-11).

The defender blocks the backfist by moving his left arm up while keeping his right arm stationary.

To defend against a side kick, all the defender has to do is pull down both arms and shove the move out of the way.

Wallace demonstrates in this sequence (1-3) the correct
way to cock the leg and throw a side kick.

If the knee is inside (1), then the correct extension on a side kick cannot be made. From a fighting stance (2), the practitioner shows the way to score with a side kick (3).

These are examples of how Wallace turns his hands, body and head to block or avoid altogether a kick or punch. By turning his shoulders (1), he can deflect a kick to the midsection or head (2). By leaning forward or back (3), he can make the kick miss completely. By leaning over and moving his shoulders in (4), his arm takes most of the punishment. Defending against a side kick (5), Wallace just keeps his arm down and his right fist against his chin. Distancing is one of Wallace's favorite ploys. Here (6), he turns away to make the kick ineffective.

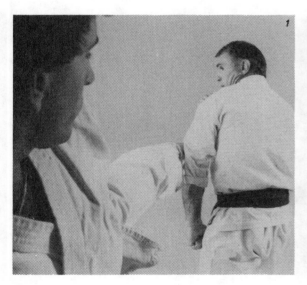

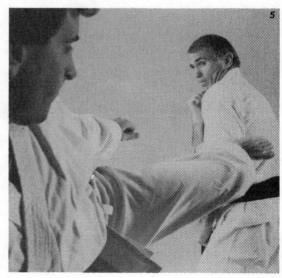

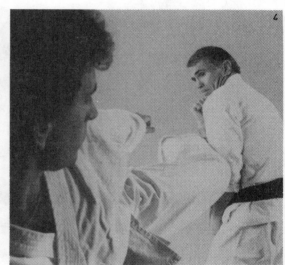

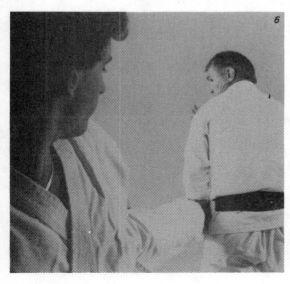

From a fighting stance (1), Wallace shows how leaning
way back (2), moving slightly to the rear (3), turning (4),
and bringing the elbow up (5) will deflect or avoid most
attacks.

Wallace's left arm does more than just hang. It serves as an integral part of his defense. In this example (1-3) Wallace shows how arm extension, when combined with a leaning action, can block most attacks.

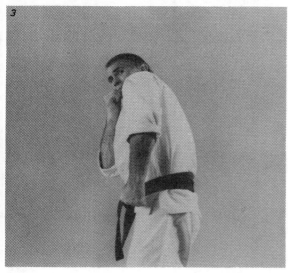

Wallace's right fist almost always hugs his chin (1-2). Even if he brings his elbow up to protect against a technique to the back of the body (3), he is covered. His chin is hidden behind the right fist and the left hand is low enough to protect against an attack to the rib area.

Wallace is facing an opponent in a Korean stance (1). He cocks for the kick (2) and then throws a roundhouse kick (3). Notice the full extension (4). He steps down (5) with a backfist, which is blocked, and he slides his rear leg up and creates an opening for a roundhouse kick low, a side kick or various hand combinations (6).

Wallace demonstrates to his assistant how he would face his opponent (1). He shows the same stance sideways (2), after which the assistant slides into a side kick (3). He helps his assistant get his knee up high for jamming techniques (4). Finally, the assistant performs the kick again with the knee higher (5).

From a ready stance (1), the attacker moves in and Wallace brings up his leg (2). Wallace then raises his knee in a jamming move (3) and fully extends the knee to prevent a possible counter (4).

Throwing one technique should create an opening somewhere else. From a ready stance (1), Wallace throws a backfist (2), which the defender is forced to block. This creates an opening to the ribs and lower stomach (3).

From a ready stance (1), the opponent throws a backfist but Wallace steps back with his right leg (2). He attempts a reverse punch (3), but is caught leaning too far forward and is hit with a defensive side kick (4).

This is what happens when you don't lean back far enough. He can hit you with the backfist (1), or he can slide up and hit you with the roundhouse kick (2-3).

HAND
TECHNIQUES

There was never anything very difficult about my hand techniques. And that's because I never had any punches that were out of the ordinary.

All I ever had was a backfist, a jab and a hook punch. My right hand was always too far back to ever be used as a weapon, although I did use it as a blocking tool. The Wallace method always was to use what I had to get in what I could.

I still wanted to develop a certain amount of power, rather than center on touch. I also made sure my defenses were up to par simply because I was sideways. When I'm sideways to my opponent, you can only see my head and left arm. Any fighter who wanted to strike another area on my body had to come around.

My punching techniques in both full-contact and point fighting were always with the left hand. It was not as much a handicap as you might think. Since I was sideways, the hook punch and the jab were natural movements. The backfist I used with my left hand down, in a circular motion. It is much like your mother's backfist or backhand when she nailed you for doing something wrong. It's a very snappy movement, it's down, it circles up, the elbow points at your partner and then the backfist snaps out. And it comes back the same way it went out. Follow the same procedure with the left hook — down, bring up the elbow, bring up the hand at the same time and hook it using your shoulders and your torque.

No matter how I attacked, I was always controlled. The key to not getting hit with a wild punch is to maintain your control, and that comes from solid hand placement. My left hand was always down and my right hand was in during point fighting. When I was fighting point tournaments, my right hand was about chest or stomach level. But as soon as I moved to full-contact fighting, the left hand came up to protect the right side of my chin. I used to lean the glove right against my cheekbone. That would protect my face, and with the elbow down, my stomach, rib and chest areas would be protected. My left arm was down, slightly bent and relaxed so if a guy did throw a hard side kick, it wouldn't injure my arm. They would see the arm down and not even concern themselves with throwing the side kick.

A lot of people tried to come down to the back of my head. All I had to do was bend over backward and the kick or punch would miss. And when they'd miss, they're within easy range of my movement.

Some of the punches used by tournament competitors are the hook punch (1), the jab (2) and the reverse punch (3).

As Wallace fakes the kick (1), the defender lowers his guard to block the blow. Wallace then counters (2) with a backfist to the head.

Faking and striking go hand-in-hand in the Wallace method. Here (1), Wallace throws a backfist strike (2) to create an opening. He recoils (3) and rather than go for another technique, he fires another backfist (4).

Again, by sliding up the roundhouse kick (1-2), he has set up his opponent for a backfist to the face (3).

The opponent is in a full-contact stance (1). Wallace applies a hook kick to the back of the head (2) which is blocked by the open hand. He then steps down (3) and adds a jab to the face (4). He coils for a backfist (5) and then executes the technique (6). He pulls back the punch and sets up for another technique (7).

Facing the traditional karate stance.

Facing the boxing-style stance.

WHAT IT TAKES TO BECOME A GOOD FIGHTER

Back when I was a student at Ball State University in Indiana, Glen Keeney, at the time one of the top fighters in the country, and me had about nine days off between each school semester. While many of the students used the vacation time to see their parents, we would take off in the car and drive as far as we could in four days.

At night, we would stop at different karate schools along the way and spar everybody in the school. Everybody. The instructor would be glad to see us, take us out to eat and let us sleep in the school that night. We'd go as far as we could in four days and then turn around and come back a different way, again stopping at karate schools.

You would be surprised at how much experience we gained from the impromptu stops. We'd fight a white belt at one school who might be the equivalent of a brown belt at another school.

The advantage was that by working with students other than our friends, we avoided becoming lackadasical, complacent. All of a sudden we didn't know what our opponent was going to throw. All of a sudden there was a sense of mystery to the sparring. Consequently, we learned more because everything was new and we were more open to different styles.

Students today lack that kind of dedication, that drive to improve. They forget you can learn from anybody. I've been nailed, and nailed good, by white belts and haven't been touched by black belts. You should use everything in your martial arts training as a learning experience.

Sometimes at my seminars I'll pair a white belt and a black belt. If you ask them to take off their belts, a lot of the time you can't tell which is which during a sparring match.

Also, when you win a match don't just be happy with the victory. Dissect the moves in your mind. Could you have used a better technique, one that would have ended the match sooner and more decisively? Did you wait too long or were you too soon with a particular move? If you have to meet him another time, how can you improve your performance?

And if you lost, rather than get upset, get into the reasons. Don't look at it as a loss, see it as a two-minute school lesson. Determine what you did wrong and how you can prevent the same thing from happening the next time around.

KARATE
AFTER 30

There is little difference in karate training when you're 16, 20, 30 or 40 years of age except the condition of the body.

Sure the speed and timing will diminish a bit, simply because of the age factor. But today I feel I'm just as strong and just as fast. Several things, however, will suffer. Timing and distance will suffer a bit, as will the healing process. A bruise that wouldn't have shown up at all a few years ago now will take three or four days to heal.

People ask me all the time: "Can I still stretch when I'm 35 or 40 years of age?" Yes, you can stretch, yes, you can do the splits, yes, you can work as hard as you normally do. Just take your time.

I still spar two to three times a week. No matter how old you are, you'll be a little slower and a little weaker than you were a year ago. But you can fill in the voids by becoming sneakier, because nothing, nothing takes the place of experience.

MEETING SOMEONE WITH A DIFFERENT STYLE

Not everybody fights the same way. If I had my way, everybody I fight would fight me left side forward because of my left leg. Their stomach is so wide open and no matter how much they protect it, I have this sneaky way of getting the little roundhouse kick into the midsection. From there, everything is open to me — the chest, the face, the back of the head, the side — and with both hand and kicking combinations. Plus it makes it a lot easier to jam and counter his movements.

If he comes charging in with a kicking technique, I can jam his movements, throw the hook punch to the face and a hook punch to the body or I can throw the backfist to the face.

Unfortunately, not every person fights the way you are most comfortable. Sometimes, you must make adjustments in the ring. You must be able to look at a fighter in the opening seconds of a match and determine if what you have can beat him. If the answer is "no," then you must go back into the recesses of your training to another option.

People who fought right side forward always gave me some trouble. At the same time, I knew enough to change my tactics. In this case, I would go with the side kick. I never was sure why the side kick worked so well against right side forward fighters, but I think it had a lot to do with the way I threw it. Their right hand or forward hand never did a good job of protecting the rib area. When this happens, let your faking techniques take over. In point tournaments, I faked a couple of side kicks and worked the roundhouse kick.

In full-contact, my best shot outside the side kick was the defensive hook kick to the face. A guy would charge in and throw a roundhouse right leg to my head. I'd just lean out of the way and counter with a left hook kick to the facial area, making sure I hit with the heel so if contact was made a lot of damage was done.

One aspect of my fighting that always screwed me up was my left hook. I wasn't very good at working the left hook to the back of the head because while I could throw it, it was never very effective on a right side forward fighter. Plus, many fighters knew throwing the punch would screw me up. And so I had to know the abilities of my opponents, if only to stay away from techniques that would put me at a decided disadvantage.

Overall, when facing an individual who fights a different style, you should be aware of what he throws, both as an offensive move and counter, how he moves, and his weaknesses.

I enjoy magazine articles where people say, "This is how I would fight Bill Wallace." I was beaten quite a few times during my point-fighting years and those who won would jam me. They wouldn't just come in and score on me because I was a very good counterfighter. What they would do, however, was counter my counter.

THE FUTURE
OF TOURNAMENT
FIGHTING

When I was a point fighter from 1967-74, you had to deliver a pretty hard shot to score a point. You couldn't just kiss the guy with your hand, you had to nail the guy. I was talking recently with a few war horses from the previous era and everybody said they threw body shots as hard as they could, while still maintaining control and balance.

The theory was, if I hit to the body my face was wide open so I needed a strong technique to keep the guy off me. When I was fighting, a point was really a point. The definition of a point was a "killing or maiming technique." It had to be a controlled killing or maiming technique to where if you did follow through with it or put full power into it, you would cause death or injury to your opponent.

Today, it's nowhere near like that. They have a new thing out called a sliding backfist. You throw the backfist first and as your arm is extended someone steps into it and you win. I'd love for you to hit somebody out on the street with that, because what you're going to do is throw the technique and pull back.

Point fighting is at a critical stage. Students learn techniques that are supposed to do damage, and then are told to use them against somebody where the rule is "you touch him before he touches you." So you throw the technique and kind of lean into it.

You don't see boxers doing that, you don't see full-contact fighters doing that, but point fighters will settle for that touch and then say, "I could have killed you." Who are you kidding? If I fall back after striking, who's off balance? Do that in a full-contact bout and you're mine because if you hit me and then fall off balance I'm going to step on you.

Also, today's fighter is not used to controlling his techniques. Back when I first started, you were allowed techniques to the face, body and groin. But you also had to show control or focusing. You could throw a punch to the face but you couldn't make contact. And since we were not wearing padding, if you did make contact you were either disqualified, warned or prepared for a counterattack.

Today, with the padding on the hands, the fighter can just throw blind techniques.

However, not everything is wrong in tournament fighting. In fact, some aspects are downright impressive. There are many more techniques nowadays. When I first began, nobody threw double or triple kicks. Most everybody threw one kick and hoped for the best. Now, they know so much more and they're not afraid to throw something. They throw jump spinning backfists, and use defensive movements that 20 years ago I never even considered, much less thought about using. Plus, they're in much better shape. In my day, a fighter would light a cigarette before a match, hand the cigarette to a friend, fight the bout and then grab the cigarette on his way out of the ring. Today, fighters work out before a bout, fight and then return to the workout room. They have combined better techniques with increased stamina.

WALLACE'S BEST SEMINAR QUESTIONS

Although I have long since retired from competitive fighting, I continue to spend the majority of my time traveling throughout the world talking about my martial arts experiences. As a regular on the martial arts seminar circuit, I am repeatedly asked about my keys to victory, my personal training regimen, today's fighters vs. yesterday's combatants.

One day I may be teaching the benefits of stretching and kicking, and the next giving advice on how to make adjustments in the ring. Since the same questions continue to come up, I think this is the perfect time to answer some of the most commonly asked seminar questions.

1) Can you learn anything from a Bill Wallace seminar?

Yes, simply because of the way I conduct my seminars. First, I talk a lot about flexibility exercises. A lot of people try to stretch, but they don't stretch correctly. There are three basic muscle groups martial artists much stretch — the quadriceps, the biceps and the hamstring group, and the abductors. Most people, however, try to stretch all three at the same time. Unfortunately, most people imitate the exercises their teachers taught them. And their teachers learned from their teachers. That doesn't necessarily mean they're the best ones, or even if they're any good at all. To stretch right, you have to work on each group individually, you have to isolate them.

Plus, I go into kicking techniques. I demonstrate how I perform the kicks — and how while they all look the same, the extension determines the success or failure of a technique.

And then I go through the isolation of different flexibility exercises; flexibility and endurance, flexibility and strength. I teach you how to be able to hold your leg in the air, how to make the leg strong and effective.

As a person works on his technique, he learns different ways of doing things. I don't say my way is the best way, the strongest way or the fastest way, but it works for me. Hopefully, a student I work with will take a little part of what I've said and incorporate it into his system.

We're not all built the same, we don't all have the same strength or the same psychological makeup. So therefore everything is going to be different. So what I teach is for each student to take a little bit and if it works for him, by all means use it. It is my gift to him.

2) Is it good for a beginning student to copy your technique?

Habits are hard to break once you're taught a basic technique for months and months and months. When you see a technique done faster, stronger and more relaxed, you come into conflict with your instructor. You go back to your training hall and your instructor tells you to do it his way. But you say that Wallace teaches something different and it helped him win. Your instructor gets upset and says doing it the "Wallace Way" will give away the technique. Well, I've been doing it one way for more than 20 years and if I'm giving it away, I'll continue to do the same.

3) Your methods appear so simple. Why have so few people been able to stop you?

From day one I had three kicks — the side kick, roundhouse kick and the hook kick — because my right leg was injured in a judo accident. My one hand technique was the backfist. Since I had to fight sideways to protect my right leg, what I had to do is develop my left side, my left leg and my left hand to where it did the job of both sides of my body. By working with it, I developed an unconscious feeling for my left side. You could never get me to turn right side forward and even if I fell down I would get up left side forward. Since I only had three kicks, I had to get what you might call "sneaky." Everybody knew what kicks were coming, but they saw them all come the same way. Since they came from the same chambering action, the same positioning, you never knew what was happening until it was too late. All I did was step in for the kick and then watch the opponent react. I reacted to your movement.

4) Can a fighter turn a weakness into a strength?

If I can do it anybody can do it. People used to say, "He can only throw three kicks," so they would try to get as close to me as they could. I'd just stick my backfist out or use the jab to pop them in the face. As they backed up, I'd kick them.

5) Despite your unorthodox fighting style, you never appeared out of control. Why?

I'm sideways. If I'm facing you and you come charging in, my first move is to back up, not come at you. When I'm sideways all I have to do is lean over. I can lean all the way to where my rear hand is touching the floor, but I'm still sideways and I can still manage a powerful kick. Look at shotokan karate fighters or people who use a boxing stance. Have them lean back and tell them to do anything. See what happens. They'll fall, they'll lose their balance, simply because their body weight goes back. My body weight is still concentrated at my hips and very low, so when I lean over the control is still there. My upper body moves but my lower body is stationary.

6) Would you have been a better fighter had you had the use of both legs?

When I was training, my instructor knew I had this disability (torn ligaments in the right knee). So when we went through the class, everybody would start left side forward and then turn right side forward. But I never made the turn. So when we first worked 15,000 kicks with the right leg and 15,000 kicks with the left leg, I just did 30,000 kicks with the left leg. I worked on side kicks, roundhouse kicks and hook kicks but no spinning kicks because I couldn't throw them with my right leg. What occurred was the assimilation of three separate angles — straight in, to the left and to the right.

7) Did one type of fighter give you the most trouble?

The fighters who gave me the most trouble were those who liked to blitz a lot. Howard Jackson immediately comes to mind. He was very fast from the opening bow. He came in like a freight train and I had trouble countering him. Working with Howard, however, helped me to keep my knee up real high. It kept him from jamming me, from getting inside and punching me. Another type of fighter who gave me trouble were those who fought right side forward, because they took away my tummy kick which set up a lot of techniques.

8) How can you tell when you are ready for competition?

If you have to feel you're ready for competition, you may never be ready. You know from the start whether you like to spar. A lot of people don't like to fight. It's true. So spar in school until you feel comfortable. You have to realize you're going to get hit sooner or later, and that when you get in front of people you may look like a jerk. Someone is going to make a fool of you sometime or another. Use everything as a learning experience. If you win, well then say, "I did good." If you lose, still look at it as a learning situation. Just play with it, and by all means have a good time.

9) What mistakes are common among beginning fighters?

The most common mistake is bowing in, having your opponent say, "I'm going to beat you," and you believing it. You actually believe it and you're beat before you ever throw a punch. Plus, a lot of new fighters use a technique I call "throw and hope." They'll take their stance and, using what their instructor said, throw a roundhouse kick. And it will probably be blocked. Now they're stumped. They have to think about what they'll throw next. They need to get away from that. Set up combinations, a master plan of plans within plans.

10) How does one make a successful adjustment from point fighting to full-contact?

In point fighting, since you don't get hit very hard it doesn't take much endurance other than being able to last two minutes in the ring. For full-contact, however, you must maintain endurance, so you'll actually have to *train* for the fight. Nothing helps when you're tired. You can be the fastest and strongest, but unless you've also got endurance, you're lost. Plus, you have to be able to take a punch as well as deliver one.

When I made the jump from point fighting to full-contact, I designed my punch to go through the body rather than just touch it. I maintained the same snap in my kicks, but rather than throw a backfist, I'd use the jab because it was a little more powerful, a little snappier. Also, I learned a little technique called the left hook. Because I'm left-handed and I fight from the left side, the left hook came easy to me. Overall, when you make the switch from point fighting to full-contact, train for endurance and technique. You can be the best technician in the world and still not be successful in the ring. I've seen guys shadowbox in the gym and they actually scare you. But the minute they put the gloves on and the bell goes "ding," they say "don't hit me, don't hit me."

11) What separated you from the host of good fighters on the circuit?

Everything kind of came natural to me. I got into it with the philosophy of never wanting to get hit. I didn't even want to get touched. Pain hurts. When I fought, I concentrated on what I could do to the individual without getting hit back. Most people will try one technique without regard to what his opponent does in return. I protected myself before the technique, during the technique and after the technique. My speed and sneakiness also came into play. I think the protection aspect, being able to defend myself against just about any technique, being able to throw effective counters, separated me from the rest.

12) Some experts contend a fundamental knowledge of martial arts techniques is not necessary in the ring. Do you agree?

No, I don't. You need the techniques for their foundation on what you later learn. You'll learn stances, the different movements, the different blocking techniques. You may never use the blocking techniques you'll learn in a traditional school, but you'll modify that knowledge to suit your individual needs.

13) Is it necessary to know the judges ahead of time?

Not so much who they are but what style they practice. A friend of mine would carry three uniforms with him to tournaments — a white traditional uniform, a white Korean uniform with black piping and a kung-fu uniform. He would go to the tournament, find out who the judges were for his event and then dress accordingly. If I'm a Korean stylist judge and you throw shotokan reverse punches and front kicks, I'm not going to call it a point. But if there is kung-fu judge and I'm wearing a kung-fu uniform, a fighter will get points based more on what he wears than what he throws. It's important to know the judges so you can prepare for what techniques will work.

14) How do you make adjustments in the ring?

The fight lasts two minutes in point tournaments, so you don't necessarily have to win the match in the first 15 seconds. When I was facing an opponent for the first time, I'd bow in and watch whether he stepped forward or backward. If we bow and he steps in, it means his weight is going to be on the front foot. If he steps back after the bow-in, his weight will be on the rear foot. If he steps forward, he might be a little aggressive. Also, I looked for where the hands were in his stance, whether he was using a left side or a right side stance, and whether he was taking a punching or kicking stance. If it was a kicking stance, you knew he had to be sideways when he kicked. If it was a punching stance, his hips had to be facing you a little bit to generate power and movement in the kicks.

I envisioned in my mind his hands, his elbows, whether he was fighting left or right side forward, whether his hips were facing me or straight to the side, and whether he was leaning back or forward. And then I'd work from there. I'd play with him, not so much to score but to see how he reacted to different techniques. I'd see how his face reacted to a kick around his head. Always look at the eyes to see if they close. Professional boxers always feel out their opponent for a round or two, so what's wrong with martial arts fighters taking 30-40 seconds to size up the other man in the ring?

15) How would you fight Bill Wallace?

What you have to do is somehow get inside me. When I'm throwing the hook kick, you have to get inside me before I make the full extension. If I get the kick out, I'll wrap it around every block you have. My only straight-line technique is the side kick, and the jab of course. If you jam my hook kick and you're fast enough to get inside the leg before I get it extended, then you've got a good chance. But then you'll never know what kick I'm throwing. Don't try to block what I throw because I'm going to throw enough junk that something's going to get in. And remember, when you block something, that means something else is open.

Some fighters tried just pounding my left side since it was always open and available. That was fine with me. I'll just absorb it. I'll let you hit me in the arm. But as I take it, I'll flow with the blow. I liked people to throw things real hard at me. As they hit me once or twice, they'd get a false sense of accomplishment. They thought they were hurting me. When they came in again, I'd lean back and suddenly they were off balance. That's when I'd counter and catch them totally off guard. Sneaky, huh?

ABOUT
THE AUTHOR

Bill Wallace retired as the undefeated Professional Karate Association middleweight champion after defeating Bill Biggs in a 12-round bout in June, 1980. The victory, Wallace's 23rd straight, signaled the end to an illustrious 15-year career in tournament and full-contact fighting.

Known to most fans simply as "Superfoot," symbolic of his dynamic left leg, which has been clocked at an excess of 60 mph, Wallace left a string of battered and bruised bodies along the karate trail by showing a kick could be the most powerful weapon in karate. He prided himself on using his foot as others would their hands, faking opponents with two or three kicks in rapid succession only to set up the real technique. His power was amazing, his precision astounding.

Even before entering the full-contact ring in 1974, Wallace was rated among the best point fighters in America for three straight years. He has won virtually every major point-fighting title at least once and boasts of multiple championships in the U.S. Championships (3 times), USKA Grandnationals (3 times) and Top Ten Nationals (2 times).

In 1973, Wallace sustained a leg injury many thought would end his career. However, one of Wallace's most famous friends, the late Elvis Presley, flew in a Los Angeles acupuncturist to treat the karate champion at Graceland Manor. Wallace, fully recovered from the injury, became the PKA middleweight champion a year later with a second-round knockout of Bernd Grothe.

A former karate, judo, wrestling and weightlifting instructor at Memphis State University, Wallace continues to be one of the most popular figures on the martial arts seminar circuit.

He also has made a big impact in the film industry. He starred with Chuck Norris in *A Force of One* and later had a small role in *Neighbors*, with John Belushi, for whom Wallace acted as bodyguard and personal trainer until the actor's death several years ago.

In a magazine interview after his retirement, Wallace said he would not return to competition karate unless the sport needed one of his patented kicks in the backside. "The only reason I would come back is if the sport starts getting sloppy. If that happens, I'll come back and try to clean it up."

And you know he could.

UNIQUE LITERARY BOOKS OF THE WORLD

Also publishers of:
Inside Karate
Inside Kung-Fu

UNIQUE PUBLICATIONS
4201 Vanowen Place
Burbank, CA 91505

PLEASE WRITE IN
FOR OUR LATEST CATALOG